YOUR KNOWLEDGE HAS VALUE

Analysis of the Controversy of a ban on Lethal Autonomous Weapons Systems (LAWS) based on the SCOT concept

Isabel Thoma

Bibliographic information published by the German National Library:

The German National Library lists this publication in the National Bibliography; detailed bibliographic data are available on the Internet at http://dnb.dnb.de.

ISBN: 9783346591562
This book is also available as an ebook.

© GRIN Publishing GmbH
Nymphenburger Straße 86
80636 München

Print and binding: Books on Demand GmbH, Norderstedt, Germany
Printed on acid-free paper from responsible sources.

The present work has been carefully prepared. Nevertheless, authors and publishers do not incur liability for the correctness of information, notes, links and advice as well as any printing errors.

GRIN web shop: https://www.grin.com/document/1170560

Analysis of the Controversy of a ban on Lethal Autonomous Weapons Systems (LAWS) based on the SCOT concept

Research Paper

Isabel Jasmin Thoma

15 December 2021

Science and Technology Studies (STS) for Development in a Global Context

MA Globalization and Development Studies

Content

Section 1: Introduction

The technology of LAWS is discussed controversially: At the political level of states, in international institutions, the scientific field of AI and robotics, the companies working in these fields, the public and the media landscape.

In 2020, *Human Rights Watch* (hrw) published a report outlining the country positions of a total of 97 states on the issue (hrw, 2020). 55 of these countries are on the *OECD*'s "DAC List of ODA Recipients" (OECD, 2020) - which is used by some as a basis for categorization as belonging to the 'Global South'[1]. The *Stop Killer Robots Campaign*, founded in 2013, lists over 180 NGOs and academic partners at international, regional and national levels, from 66 different countries (Stop Killer Robots, 2021). In addition, there are statements of associations, which state their position towards the technology of autonomous weapons, for example, the *Non-Aligned Movement*, a forum of 120 developing countries (NAM, 2021), or *NATO* (NATO, 2021). All this shows that the technology of LAWS does not only affect the countries where the manufacturers or buyers of the weapons are located – which is mostly countries considered to be from the 'Global North', but at the same time also those states in which the weapons are already in use and will be in the future, i.e. warring states, which are largely assigned to the 'Global South' according to the *OECD* list. The issue, however, potentially affects everyone because the weapons could be used anywhere and raise ethical and humanitarian questions that affect the entire global society.

This paper aims to shed light on the question: *How is the globally discussed technology of LAWS and its ban perceived by different social groups?* Currently, those who are against a ban dominate globally. These are powerful countries that are also leaders in the development of LAWS and refer to the justifications of experts and commercial players. The German focus

---

[1] 'Global South' is used in social sciences as a politically correct substitute for formerly common terms like 'Third World' or 'underdeveloped' since it is supposedly less colonialist and hierarchical. However, the North/South distinction also insinuates, in my view, a weighting meaning. Uniform definitions of the term 'Global South' do not exist. Instead, there are different concepts. Personally, I am close to an interpretation of Alfred López, who describes the 'Global South' as a group of global subalterns: "The global South also marks the mutual recognition among the world's subalterns of their shared condition at the margins of the brave new neoliberal world of globalization" (López, 2007, p. 1). The 'Global South' according to López is thus not a list of nation states, but disempowered humans who are socially, politically and intellectually disadvantaged by neoliberal policies. In the context of whether LAWS are a case that includes the Global South, I answer yes. For I argue that it is primarily these subalterns who suffer the negative consequences of the technology if it remains unchecked.

in this paper is due to the author's personal connection to Germany as well as the fact that the topic is currently on the agenda there in the context of the new government formation.

In the following (Section 2), the controversy of banning LAWS is embedded in the scientific discourse on risk and uncertainty and a selection of the concepts is applied to the technology to not only emphasize the socio-political relevance mentioned in the introduction, but also the academic relevance. Next, the methodological concept of SCOT is introduced theoretically (Section 3) and then applied to the LAWS object of study (Section 4). Finally, the conclusion (Section 5) summarizes the main findings, highlights the limitations of the work, and suggests a way forward.

Section 2: Risk and Uncertainty in STS

Risk and uncertainty are part of modern life. In this context, Ulrich Beck coined the term "world risk society" (Beck, 2006). In particular, technological risks are the focus of global discourse. Technologies create new industrial opportunities that trigger changes beyond the local context thanks to globalization. If the risks of these innovative technologies are overestimated, they can block their development and thus progress in general. If the risks are underestimated, however, unforeseen consequences can cause irreversible damage. (Juma & Yee-Cheong, 2005, p. 174-175)

What exactly does the term risk describe? Some definitions consider risk as an objective component of something, others consider risk as the result of a social process - for example Boholm, who describes risk as "a relational term that emerges out of contexts depending on shared conventionally established meanings, that is to say, 'culture'" (2003, p. 175). According to him, risk consists of the connection of the origin of potential harm (the technology of LAWS) with the object at risk (potentially every human) and the evaluation of consequences (the different ways LAWS are being seen as). Risk is thus a "relational order through which connections between people, 'things' and 'outcomes' are constituted" (Boholm, 2003, p. 175).

In the context of how we can deal with uncertainty, Asselt and Renn distinguish so-called "simple risks" from "systemic risks" (2011, p. 436). Simple risks are those for which statistics exist and that recur and can therefore be calculated as a linear function of probability and effect. Systemic risks require a holistic approach, are characterized by ripple and spillover effects, and affect areas that are themselves characterized by risk. For example, LAWS technology has an impact not only on the weapons industry, but also the sciences of AI and robotics, the economy of a state, and political matters. This makes risk governance complex and unwieldy. Despite the lack of scientific evidence, decision-making regarding such risks is mostly technocratic, i.e., decision-makers rely on expert judgments and recommendations to specify the course of actions. This is what Asselt and Vos call the "uncertainty paradox: an umbrella term for situations in which uncertainty is present and acknowledged, but the role of science is framed as one of providing certainty" (2008, p. 282). In practice, it is common for policymakers to make decisions without having all the answers. This is also true for LAWS. Although the technology is still in development and no one can foresee what the consequences will be for the global community, national governments find themselves forced to make decisions. This is the case in Germany, for example, where three big parties agreed in their coalition agreement on 24.11.21 to allow the acquisition of armed drones to protect their own soldiers (Koalitionsvertrag, p. 149). However, the coalition rejects LAWS which are completely beyond the control of humans and advocates an international ban on them (Koalitionsvertrag, p. 145).

Risk and uncertainty are relevant topics in science and generate an academic discourse that offers direct implications for action and practical applications. After a short theoretical introduction to the methodological concept SCOT, this will be further exemplified by the technology of LAWS and the controversy surrounding a ban of the same.

Section 3: Methodological Concept of SCOT

SCOT is a multidirectional approach characterized by the interplay of variation and selection (Pinch & Bijker, 1987, p. 22). The technological artifact or the socio-technical complex is thus examined for its "interpretative flexibility" (Pinch & Bijker, 1987, p. 22), meaning it is examined which variants of the object endure and which are abandoned during the selection process. Therefore, in the first step of the analysis, social groups are identified and described in detail, which have a relationship to the object of study. Further, the problems of each of such groups in relation to the object are considered. Doing so, it may be that a group is not homogeneous in its attitude and therefore must be divided into separate groups (Pinch & Bijker, 1987, p. 27). In focusing on each group's problems with the artifact, diverse conflicts become known, which may result in diverse approaches to solving the problem. Concluding, in the first step the interpretative flexibility is traced, i.e., it is shown that technological complexes are culturally constructed and interpreted. In the second step of the analysis closure mechanisms are shown, i.e., "the stabilization of an artifact and the 'disappearance' of problems" (Pinch & Bijker, 1987, p. 37). Crucial is not whether the problem has been solved, but whether the social groups regard it as such.

In conclusion, SCOT is a descriptive method that describes technologies through the attributions of all relevant social groups. These groups, in turn, are shaped by social, cultural, and political norms and values, which are reflected in the attributions. Which social groups are relevant in the context of LAWS, which perspectives and problems they project onto the technology and which solutions this could produce will be examined next. It is not possible to conduct an all-encompassing analysis within the scope of this paper since LAWS is not a single technological artifact but a socio-technical complex with actors involved all over the world. Nevertheless, the foundation for more comprehensive analyses will be laid and the SCOT method will be demonstrated in its application.

Section 4: Analysis of the Controversy of a ban on LAWS

In the following, it will be examined how the controversy surrounding a ban of LAWS is developing. The different meanings that social groups ascribe to the technology serve as a structuring device. Various groups identify risks and have different attitudes toward the technology, its ban and approaches to how it should be dealt with. Although the controversy is to be viewed from a 'German perspective', in today's globalized world this includes actors and perspectives worldwide. For it is also relevant for Germany how other states position themselves, what institutions such as the UN and other NGOs announce, what the international scientific community publishes and how the world market and the development of technology is promoted worldwide. Thus, before specifically German actors and their perspectives can be examined, it is essential to gain a sense of the overall situation worldwide. That is what this work is intended to contribute to.

What complicates discussions on LAWS is that it is a collective term for various weapon systems with autonomous functions with no uniform international definition. LAWS can be air defense weapons, cluster munitions and missiles, armed drones, anti-personnel weapons, mobile ground weapon systems, or mobile surface water and underwater weapon systems. Nevertheless, an attempt will be made to look at the technology at large, as well as the key players and their positions towards a ban.

4

Overall, a range of actors engage in the controversy which can be categorized in different ways: As with any product, two important stakeholder groups are the producers and the users. In the case of LAWS as a technology full of risks and uncertainties, according to Asselt and Vos, the actors can also be divided into "*risk producers*," "*risk assessors*," "*risk managers*," and "*risk protesters*" (2008, p. 283). To some extent, these two category systems overlap. Then again, there are actors that do not fall into any of the mentioned categories. Figure 1 shows those categories plus the respective groups of actors.

LETHAL AUTONOMOUS WEAPON SYSTEMS (LAWS)

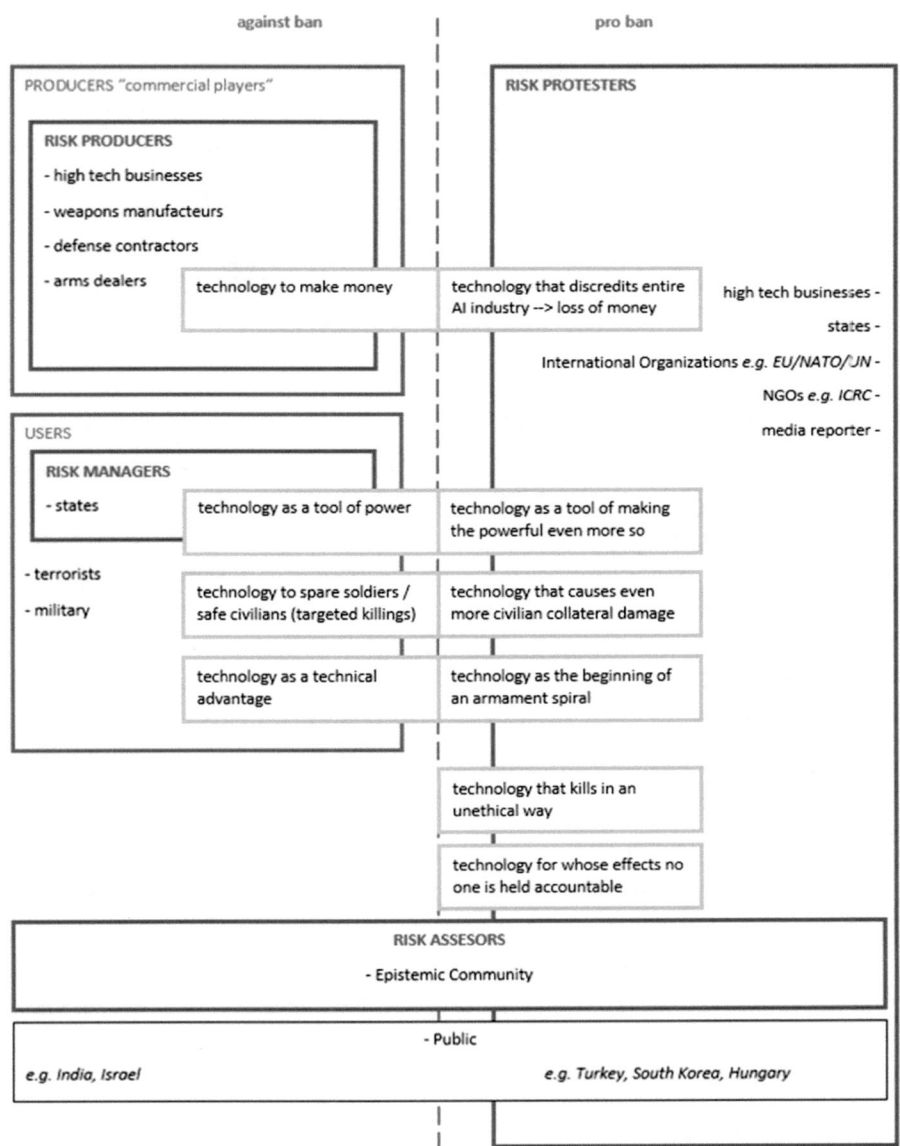

Figure 1: Selection of the most relevant actors in the controversy of a ban on LAWS and their views of the technology.

Looking at LAWS through the eyes of IT companies, most see them as a threat to their industry. So much so that over 130 major tech companies spoke out against the military use of AI and robotics in an open letter. It was not the first time such a letter has been published in the run-up to the International Joint Conference on Artificial Intelligence (IJCAI) - the world's most prestigious AI conference held biennially in odd-numbered years since 1969. The difference in 2017 was that the signatories were not primarily researchers from universities as two years earlier, but experts and representatives of AI and robotics companies from 26 different countries. Among them were names like Elon Musk, Mustafa Suleyman or Ryan Hickman and Soohyun Bae. As companies that are themselves researching and working on the very technology that could be used to develop LAWS, their letter calls on the UN to ban them. Their fear:

> "Once developed, they will permit armed conflict to be fought at a scale greater than ever, and at timescales faster than humans can comprehend. These can be weapons of terror, weapons that despots and terrorists use against innocent populations, and weapons hacked to behave in undesirable ways." (Open Letter, 2017)

The concern is that the technology could fall into the wrong hands, be manipulated, be used for unethical purposes, spiral out of control, and discredit the entire AI and robotics industry. But, at the same time, there are companies that may very well be working on military contracts and making good money doing so. Like ClearPath Robotics, which continues to collaborate with its military clients even though it pledged its endorsement of the ban. Or Google, which ultimately voted in favor of the ban, but before that bought Boston Dynamics, which had close ties to the US military, for commercial purposes. (Hynek & Solovyeva, 2020)

Another important group of actors in the controversy about LAWS are the states, which can be found in the group of users and risk managers on the one hand, and the group of risk protesters on the other. Since 2013, 30 countries[2] have called for a ban on LAWS. In contrast, countries such as China, Israel, Russia, South Korea, the UK, and the US are investing heavily in the development of LAWS (hrw, 2020, p. 3). Furthermore, the world's top leaders in LAWS development include countries like France, Germany, Sweden or Italy. All these countries, benefiting from the arms exports, refrain from publicly opposing the LAWS technology - in contrast to the less technologically developed states mentioned above (Hynek & Solovyeva,

---

[2] „Algeria, Argentina, Austria, Bolivia, Brazil, Chile, China, Colombia, Costa Rica, Cuba, Djibouti, Ecuador, Egypt, El Salvador, Ghana, Guatemala, Holy See, Iraq, Jordan, Mexico, Morocco, Namibia, Nicaragua, Pakistan, Panama, Peru, State of Palestine, Uganda, Venezuela, and Zimbabwe" (hrw, 2020).

2020, p. 86). While the countries without the possibility of entering the development of LAWS consider the technology as a tool of making the powerful even more powerful, for the dominant states it represents a pursuit of power and wealth.

When considering IOs, it is not surprising that the UN, for example, has not yet agreed on restrictive measures and rules regarding LAWS. The great actors in the global decision-making process block UN bodies such as the CCW. The UNSG, Antonio Guterres, however endorsed a ban, challenging the opposition within the UN. In a 2018 speech, he says,

> "I sincerely believe that technological developments are a major ally in the implementation of our 2030 Agenda for Sustainable Development. (…) In the Data Age, we must find a balance between innovation and regulation. (…) My disarmament agenda underscores the urgency and necessity of paying attention to the military uses of new technologies. Imagine the consequences of an autonomous system that could, by itself, target and attack human beings. I call upon States to ban these weapons, which are politically unacceptable and morally repugnant." (Guterres, 2018)

IOs such as the OSCE or the European Parliament (EP) also support a ban on LAWS based on ethical concerns and "the importance of human control on life and death decisions" (Hynek & Solovyeva, 2020, p. 86).

For reasons of space, only one other group of actors will be mentioned: NGOs. Like the IOs, faith leaders, various Nobel Peace Prize laureates and some states, NGOs related to the topic are in favor of a ban on LAWS. And even if, according to the distribution of power, there is currently no majority for a pro-ban movement, the power of NGOs should not be underestimated. They are skilled in campaigns such as those to ban cluster munitions, anti-personnel landmines or nuclear weapons. Through discursive tools, they can shape narratives, steer the discourse, create publicity, inform the public, and ultimately build normative pressure and assert moral authority. They are driven by a desire to support the public interest, improve human welfare and exert influence on governments and non-state actors. The ICRC as a key humanitarian actor among NGOs shall be highlighted. It operates internationally, has IO-equivalent status, maintains relations with the private sector, engages in political lobbying, and monitors compliance with the Geneva Laws and IHL. Regarding LAWS, the ICRC expresses concern about the loss of human control:

> "The use of autonomous weapon systems entails risks due to the difficulties in anticipating and limiting their effects. This loss of human control and judgment in the use of force and weapons raises serious concerns from humanitarian, legal and ethical perspectives." (ICRC, 2021)

To address the problem, the ICRC advocates internationally agreed limits: "Beyond new legal rules, these limits may also include common policy standards and good practice guidance, which can be complementary and mutually reinforcing" (ICRC, 2021).

In Germany, a coalition of the SPD, the Greens and the FDP has been in power since 8.12.21. The role of the Greens is particularly interesting with regard to questions on the topic of LAWS, as they have always been considered a pacifist party. In this context, a Green politician was interviewed prior to this work, who confirmed that with the prospect of government participation, the Greens are moving away from their radical position and showing a willingness to compromise with regard to the expansion and use of LAWS. This is because in Germany, the use of drones cannot be responsibly failed at the given time. For example, the Bundeswehr has long called for drones to be authorized not only for surveillance purposes, but also as armed drones to protect their own soldiers. However, it remains to be seen what developments will be pursued under the new government and how Germany will position itself in the debate on LAWS and a possible ban on them.

As things stand, the structural distribution of power leads to few dominant actors controlling the situation and driving the unregulated development of LAWS. Nevertheless, there is a growing acceptance that regulation and control is necessary in view of the rapid development of LAWS technology and is ultimately in the interest of all. What the regulations might look like in concrete terms is of secondary importance at this point in the debate. In the first place, it is a matter of agreeing in general that regulations are necessary. To reach a consensus, however, it can of course be beneficial to make specific proposals to the other side so that compromises can be found.

Section 5: Conclusion

As the analysis has shown, the controversy is far from over and all actors are still searching for solutions. Nevertheless, this paper aims to provide an entry point into the SCOT analysis of LAWS technology and the global controversy surrounding a ban on it. For this purpose, the technology was framed by the academic discourse on risk and uncertainty. As analysis concept, SCOT was proposed. The analysis conducted thereafter initially focused on defining relevant social groups and placing and categorizing them within the overall concept. A closer look at the individual social groups revealed their perspectives on the technology. Further research would have to address the issue of problem solving in more detail to identify possible closure mechanisms. This is further complicated by the fact that the controversy surrounding LAWS is still far from stabilization and the problems associated with it have not yet been solved and therefore cannot be analyzed retrospectively. In this context, further work could go deeper and shed light on the content-related solutions proposed by the individual actors. For the sake of completeness, it is also necessary to examine other actors in the controversy that are only hinted at in the figure but not further explained in the text. Despite these limitations of the present work, it could be shown that it is worthwhile to look at the controversy using the SCOT method to trace not only what ultimately happens to a technology, but to understand what is selected, rejected, or reinforced along the way and why.

Reference List

An Open Letter to the United Nations Convention on Certain Conventional Weapons. (2017). Future of Life Institute. https://futureoflife.org/autonomous-weapons-open-letter-2017/

Asselt, M. B. A. van & Renn, O. (2011). Risk Governance. Journal of Risk Research, 14(4), 431–449. DOI: https://doi.org/10.1080/13669877.2011.553730

Asselt, M. B. A. van & Vos, E. (2008). Wrestling with uncertain risks: EU regulation of GMOs and the uncertainty paradox. Journal of Risk Research, 11(1-2), 281-300. https://doi.org/10.1080/13669870801990806

Beck, U. (2006). Living in the world risk society. Economy and Society, 35(3), 329-345. DOI: https://doi.org/10.1080/03085140600844902

Bijker, W. E. (2015). Technology, Social Construction of. In J. D. Wright (ed.), *International Encyclopedia of the Social & Behavioral Sciences* (pp. 135-140). Elsevier. DOI: https://doi.org/10.1016/B978-0-08-097086-8.85038-2

Boholm, A. (2003). The cultural nature of risk: Can there be an anthropology of uncertainty? Ethnos, 68(2), 159-178. DOI: https://doi.org/10.1080/0014184032000097722

Guterres, A. (2018, Sep 11). *Secretary-General's Address to the Paris Peace Forum.* United Nations. https://www.un.org/sg/en/content/sg/statement/2018-11-11/allocution-du-secr%C3%A9taire-g%C3%A9n%C3%A9ral-au-forum-de-paris-sur-la-paix

Human Rights Watch. (2020). *Stopping Killer Robots. Country Positions on Banning Fully Autonomous Weapons and Retaining Human Control.* https://www.hrw.org/report/2020/08/10/stopping-killer-robots/country-positions-banning-fully-autonomous-weapons-and#_ftn8

Hynek, N. & Solovyeva, A. (2020). Operations of power in autonomous weapon systems: ethical conditions and socio-political prospects. *AI & Society*, 36, 79-99. https://doi.org/10.1007/s00146-020-01048-1

International Committee of the Red Cross. (2021, May 12). *ICRC position on autonomous weapon systems.* ICRC. https://www.icrc.org/en/document/icrc-position-autonomous-weapon-systems

Juma, C. & Yee-Cheong, L. (2005). Innovation: Applying knowledge in development. UN Millennium Project. Task Force on Science, Technology, and Innovation. UNDP.

Koalitionsvertrag zwischen SPD, Bündnis90/Die Grünen und FDP. (2021). Mehr Fortschritt wagen. Bündnis für Freiheit, Gerechtigkeit und Nachhaltigkeit. [Daring more progress. Alliance for Freedom, Justice and Sustainability.] https://www.spd.de/koalitionsvertrag2021/

López, A. J. (2007, Winter). The (Post) Global South. *The Global South*, 1(1), 1-11. https://www.jstor.org/stable/40339224

NAM. (2021). Working paper to be submitted by the Bolivarian Republic of Venezuela on behalf of the Non-Aligned Movement (NAM) and Other States Parties to the Convention on

Certain Conventional Weapons (CCW). https://www.google.com/url?sa=t&rct=j&q=&
esrc=s&source=web&cd=&ved=2ahUKEwjy-9OlirH0AhWJ2aQKHZodA3MQFnoECAI
QAQ&url=https%3A%2F%2Fdocuments.unoda.org%2Fwp-content%2Fuploads%2F202
%2F06%2FNAM.pdf&usg=AOvVaw1IGm2NwgXkREuKtYT9wSPb

NATO. (2021, Oct 22). *Emerging and disruptive technologies.* North Atlantic Treaty
Organization. https://www.nato.int/cps/en/natohq/topics_184303.htm

OECD. (2020). DAC List of ODA Recipients. https://www.oecd.org/dac/financing-sustaina
ble-development/development-finance-standards/DAC-List-ODA-Recipients-for-reporting
-2021-flows.pdf

Pinch, T. J. & Bijker, W. E. (1987). The Social Construction of Facts and Artifacts: Or How
the Sociology of Science and the Sociology of Technology Might Benefit Each Other. In:
W. E. Bijker, T. Hughes & T. Pinch (eds.), *The Social Construction of Technological
Systems. New Directions in the Sociology and History of Technology* (pp. 11-44). The MIT
Press. Stable URL: http://www.jstor.com/stable/j.ctt5vjrsq.8

Stop Killer Robots. (2021). *Our member organisations.* Stop Killer Robots.
https://www.stopkillerrobots.org/a-global-push/member-organisations/

YOUR KNOWLEDGE HAS VALUE

- We will publish your bachelor's and master's thesis, essays and papers

- Your own eBook and book - sold worldwide in all relevant shops

- Earn money with each sale

Upload your text at www.GRIN.com
and publish for free